CONTENTS

Where did the Earth come from?

The Earth came from a cloud of dust. The dust whizzed around the Sun at speed and began to stick together to form lumps of rock. The rocks crashed into each other to make the planets. The Earth is one of these planets.

A cloud of dust spun around the Sun

Why does the Moon look lumpy?

Big rocks from space, called meteorites, have crashed into the Moon and made dents on its surface. These dents are called craters and they give the Moon a lumpy appearance.

Lumps of rock began to form

The Earth was formed from the lumps of rock →

What is the Earth made of?

The Earth is a huge ball-shaped lump of rock. Most of the Earth's surface is covered by water – this makes the seas and oceans. Rock that is not covered by water makes the land.

Face the Moon!

The Moon travels around the Earth. As the Moon doesn't spin, we only ever see one side of its surface.

Why does the Earth spin?

Morning

The Earth is always spinning. This is because it was made from a spinning cloud of gas and dust. As it spins, the Earth leans a little to one side. It takes the Earth 24 hours to spin around once. This period of time is called a day.

Evening

Discover

There are 24 hours in a day. How many minutes are there in one hour?

Spinning Earth

4

Hot and cold!

In the Caribbean, the sea can be as warm as a bath. In the Arctic, it is so cold, that the sea freezes over.

Why do we have day and night?

Mid-day

The Sun

Every day, each part of the Earth spins towards the Sun, and then away from it. When a part of the Earth is facing the Sun, it is daytime there. When that part is facing away from Earth, it is night time.

Night

Do people live on the Moon?

No they don't. There is no air on the Moon so people cannot live there. Astronauts have visited the Moon in space rockets. They wear special equipment to help them breathe.

What is inside the Earth?

Crust

There are different layers inside the Earth. There is a thin, rocky crust, a solid area called the mantle and a centre called the core. The outer part of the core is made of hot, liquid metal. The inner core is made of solid metal.

Natural magnet!

Near the centre of the Earth is hot, liquid iron. As the Earth spins, the iron behaves like a magnet. This is why a compass needle points to North and South.

Can we travel into the Earth?

No, we can't. The Earth's core is incredibly hot and so far down that no one could ever go there. Sometimes, boiling-hot liquid rock bursts up through the Earth's surface from mountains called volcanoes.

Inner core

Outer core

Mantle

Which way?

Use a compass to find out which direction is North. Move around holding your compass, does the needle move?

Does the ground move?

The Earth's crust is split into huge areas called plates. Each plate is moving very slowly. If the plates move apart from each other they may cause earthquakes. If they move towards each other they may form volcanoes or mountains.

What is a fossil?

A trilobite was an ancient sea creature

A fossil was once a living thing that has now turned to stone. By studying fossils, scientists can learn more about the past and how animals, such as dinosaurs, used to live.

Scientists digging up and studying fossils

How is a fossil made?

It takes millions of years to make a fossil. When an animal dies, it may be buried by sand. The soft parts of its body rot away, leaving just bones, teeth or shells. These slowly turn to rock and a fossil has formed.

Find

Look for rocks in your garden. They may be so old dinosaurs could have trodden on them.

1. The trilobite dies

2. The trilobite gets covered with mud

3. The mud turns to stone

House of stones!

In Turkey, some people live in caves. These huge cone-shaped rocks stay very cool in the hot weather.

4. The fossil forms inside the stone

Why do rocks crumble?

When a rock is warmed up by the Sun it gets a little bigger. When it cools down, the rock shrinks to its original size. If this process happens to a rock too often, it starts to crumble away.

What is a volcano?

A volcano is a mountain that sometimes shoots hot, liquid rock out of its top. Deep inside a volcano is an area called a magma chamber. This is filled with liquid rock. If pressure builds up in the chamber, the volcano may explode, and liquid rock will shoot out of the top.

Erupting volcano

Liquid rock

Magma chamber

10

What is a range?

A range is the name for a group of mountains. The biggest ranges are the Alps in Europe, the Andes in South America, the Rockies in North America and the highest of all – the Himalayas in Asia.

How are mountains made?

One way that mountains are formed is when the Earth's plates crash together. The crust at the edge of the plates slowly crumples and folds. Over millions of years this pushes up mountains. The Himalayan Mountains in Asia were made this way.

Mountain range is pushed up

Layer on layer

When a volcano erupts, the hot lava cools and forms a rocky layer. With each new eruption, another layer is added and the volcano gets bigger.

11

Why are there earthquakes?

Earthquakes happen when the plates in the Earth's crust move apart suddenly, or rub together. They start deep underground in an area called the focus. The land above the focus is shaken violently. The worst part of the earthquake happens above the focus, in an area called the epicentre.

Epicentre

Remember

Can you remember what breaks at level 5 on the Richter Scale? Read these pages again to refresh your memory.

Focus

12

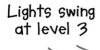

Lights swing at level 3

Windows break at level 5

Bridges and buildings collapse at level 7

What is The Richter Scale?

The Richter Scale measures the strength of an earthquake. It starts at number one and goes up to number eight. The higher the number, the more powerful and destructive the earthquake.

Super senses!

Some people believe that animals can sense when an earthquake is about to happen!

Can earthquakes start fires?

Yes, a powerful earthquake can cause fires. In 1906, a huge earthquake in San Francisco, USA caused lots of fires. The fires burnt down most of the city and the people who lived there became homeless.

What is a glacier?

Glaciers are huge rivers of ice found near the tops of mountains. Snow falls on the mountain and becomes squashed to make ice. The ice forms a glacier that slowly moves down the mountainside until it melts.

Moving glacier

Fancy flakes!

Snowflakes are made of millions of tiny crystals. No two snowflakes are the same because the crystals make millions of different shapes.

Melted ice

Can ice be fun?

Yes, it can! Many people go ice skating and they wear special boots with blades on them called ice skates. Figure skaters are skilled athletes who compete to win prizes.

What is an iceberg?

Icebergs are big chunks of ice that have broken off glaciers and drifted into the sea. Only a small part of the iceberg can be seen above the water. The main part of the iceberg is hidden under the water.

Iceberg

Look

Next time it snows, put some gloves on and let the snowflakes fall into your hand. Can you see crystals?

Where do rivers flow to?

Rivers flow to the sea or into lakes. They start off as small streams in hills and mountains. The streams flow downhill, getting bigger and wider. The place where a river meets the sea, or flows into a lake, is called the river mouth.

Oxbow lake

River mouth

Why are there waterfalls?

Waterfalls are made when water wears down rocks to make a cliff face. The water then falls over the edge into a deep pool called a plunge pool. Waterfalls may only be a few centimetres high, or several hundred metres high!

Discover

Try to find out the name of the highest waterfall in the world. Where is it?

16

A river begins in the mountains

Meander

Risky business!

Salmon are a type of fish. Every year, fishermen try to catch them as they swim back to the river they were born in to have their babies.

What is a lake?

A lake is a big area of water that is surrounded by land. Some lakes are so big that they are called inland seas. Most lake water is fresh rather than salty. The biggest lake in the world is the Caspian Sea in Asia.

Lake

How are caves made?

When rain falls on rock, it can make caves. Rainwater mixes with a gas in the air called carbon dioxide. This makes a strong acid. This acid can attack the rock and make it disappear. Underground, the rainwater makes caves in which streams and lakes can be found.

Underground cave

Lava cave

Can lava make caves?

When a volcano erupts and lava flows through the mountain, it can carve out a cave. A long time after the eruption, when the volcano is no longer active, people can walk through this lava cave without having to bend down.

What is a stalactite?

Rocky spikes that hang from cave ceilings are called stalactites. When water drips from the cave ceiling, it leaves tiny amounts of a rocky substance behind. Very slowly, over a long period of time, this grows into a stalactite.

Super spiky!

Stalagmites grow up from the cave floor. Dripping water leaves a rocky substance that grows into a rocky spike.

Is there water in the desert?

Yes there is. Deserts sometimes get rain. This rainwater seeps into the sand and collects in rock. The water then builds up and forms a pool called an oasis. Plants grow around the oasis and animals visit the pool to drink.

Oasis

What are grasslands?

Grasslands are found when there is too much rain for a desert but not enough rain for a forest. Large numbers of animals can be found living and feeding on grasslands, including zebras, antelopes and lions.

Draw

Create a picture of a camel crossing a desert – don't forget to include its wide feet!

Big feet!

Camels have wide feet that stop them sinking into the sand. They can also store water in their bodies for a long time.

Rainforest

What is a rainforest?

In hot places, such as South America, grow areas of thick, green forest. These are rainforests, and they are home to many amazing plants and animals. Rainforests have rainy weather all year round.

Where does rain come from?

Rain comes from the ocean! Water moves between the ocean, air and land in a water cycle. A fine mist of water rises into the air from the ocean and from plants. This fine mist then forms clouds. Water can fall from the clouds as rain.

Water falls from clouds as rain

Water cycle

Stormy weather!
Every day there are more than 45,000 thunderstorms on the Earth! Thunderstorms are most common in tropical places, such as Indonesia.

22

How does a tornado start?

A tornado is the fastest wind on Earth. Tornadoes
start over very hot ground. Here, warm air rises
quickly and makes a spinning funnel. This funnel
acts like a vacuum cleaner, destroying buildings
and lifting cars and lorries off the ground.

Tornado

A fine mist of
water rises from
the ocean

Do storms have eyes?

Yes, storms do have eyes! A hurricane is a very
dangerous storm. The centre of a hurricane is
called the eye and here it is completely still.
However, the rest of the storm can reach
speeds of up to 300 kilometres an hour.

23

Index

First published in 2007 by
Miles Kelly Publishing Ltd,
Harding's Barn, Bardfield End Green,
Thaxted, Essex, CM6 3PX, UK

Copyright © Miles Kelly Publishing Ltd 200

This edition published 2013

2 4 6 8 10 9 7 5 3 1

Publishing Director Belinda Gallagher
Creative Director Jo Cowan
Assistant Editor Lucy Dowling
Volume Designer Sally Lace
Cover Designer Jo Cowan
Production Manager Elizabeth Collir
Reprographics Stephan Davis,
Lorraine King
Character Cartoonist Mike Foster

ISBN 978-1-78209-428-9

Printed in China

British Library Cataloguing-in-Publication D
A catalogue record for this book is availa
from the British Library

ACKNOWLEDGEMENTS
All artwork from the Miles Kelly Artwork Ba

The publishers would like to thank
janrysavy/istockphoto.com for the use of
their cover photograph

All other photographs are from:
Corel, digitalSTOCK, digitalvision, John Fox
PhotoAlto, PhotoDisc, PhotoEssentials, Photc
Stockbyte

Every effort has been made to acknowledge
source and copyright holder of each pictur
Miles Kelly Publishing apologises for any
unintentional errors or omissions.

Made with paper from a sustainable fores

www.mileskelly.net
info@mileskelly.net